THE GLOBAL GUIDE TO MYTHOLOGY

A Guide to GREEK Myths

By Johanna Barrow

Cavendish Square

Published in 2025 by Cavendish Square Publishing, LLC
2544 Clinton Street Buffalo, NY 14224

Website: cavendishsq.com

Cataloging-in-Publication Data

Names: Barrow. Johanna.
Title: A guide to Greek myths / Johanna Barrow.
Description: Buffalo, NY : Cavendish Square Publishing, 2025. | Series: The global guide to mythology | Includes glossary and index.
Identifiers: ISBN 9781502672186 (pbk.) | ISBN 9781502672193 (library bound) | ISBN 9781502672209 (ebook)
Subjects: LCSH: Mythology, Greek–Juvenile literature. | Gods, Greek–Juvenile literature. | Goddesses, Greek–Juvenile literature.
Classification: LCC BL783.B369 2025 | DDC 292.1'3–dc23

Editor: Jennifer Lombardo
Copyeditor: Rachael Morlock
Designer: Deanna Lepovich

The photographs in this book are used by permission and through the courtesy of: Cover image AI generated by The Rosen Publishing Group using Midjourney; cover, footer, pp. 10, 18, 27, 36 (graphic element) berkah jaya material/Shutterstock.com; back cover, pp. 1, 3, 4, 5, 6, 7, 9, 13, 17, 21, 25, 30, 35, 41, 42, 43, 44, 45, 46, 47, 48 (graphic element) Marylia/Shutterstock.com; p. 5 Peter Hermes Furian/Shutterstock.com; p. 6 pipojackman/Shutterstock.com; p. 8 Milagli/Shutterstock.com; p. 11 World History Archive/Alamy Stock Photo; p. 14 Leonard Zhukovsky/Shutterstock.com; p. 15 turtix/Shutterstock.com; p. 16 wabeno/Shutterstock.com; p. 19 Gilmanshin/Shutterstock.com; p. 20 Greece, 4th century BC - Stater- Ares (reverse) - 1917.995.b - Cleveland Museum of Art/Wikimedia Commons; p. 22 Jean Lepautre, Minerva Changing Arachne into a Spider, published 1676, NGA 70435/Wikimedia Commons; p. 24 7Island/Shutterstock.com; p. 26 Hercules Capturing Cerberus from The Labors of Hercules MET DP841145/Wikimedia Commons; p. 28 Hyléos et Rhoécos/Wikimedia Commons; p. 30 Arthur Balitskii/Shutterstock.com; p. 31 Polyphemos-MuseumOfFineArtsBoston-March25-07/Wikimedia Commons; p. 34 Kamira/Shutterstock.com; p. 37 Kurt Vansteelant/Shutterstock.com; p. 38 Grafissimo/iStock Photo; p. 40 lucarista/Shutterstock.com.

CPSIA compliance information: Batch #CSCSQ25: For further information contact Cavendish Square Publishing LLC at 1-877-980-4450.

Printed in the United States of America

CONTENTS

INTRODUCTION

In addition to the lands we know as Greece today, ancient Greece included parts of what are now Türkiye and Italy. In the country's earliest days, it was divided into small, individually governed areas called city-states. City-states were often separated by forests or mountains and were far apart, and the **dialects** spoken in each city-state varied. As a result, each city-state generally had its own myths or versions of myths.

Although the ancient Greeks did not invent mythology, their myths became very popular as Greek influence spread around the world. Starting in the fourth century BCE, Alexander the Great (the king of Macedonia, which was a kingdom that originated on part of the Greek peninsula) began invading other countries. His successes brought Greeks together politically. Some city-states began to work together, sometimes against a common enemy. By that time, they also shared a common language. People began to travel and move to other city-states. They also began to travel outside of Greece. This travel helped spread Greek myths and other parts of their culture.

The word "myth" comes from the Greek word *mythos*, which literally means "story." However, myths were much

This map shows Greece as it looks today, surrounded by its neighbors. (The official name of the country of Macedonia is North Macedonia.) The ancient Greek Empire reached beyond modern borders.

more than simple stories to ancient cultures; they were an important part of life. Everyday life was not always easy in ancient Greece. People did not live as long as they do now. Life was more difficult, with no modern conveniences such as air conditioning or running water. The hardships in their daily lives led the ancient Greeks to look to their deities, or gods and goddesses, for help. The stories about these deities were passed from person to person and from generation to generation.

Each culture creates myths that reflect its beliefs, which are often a result of its circumstances. For example, myths

This statue of Poseidon sits underwater off the coast of San Andrés Island, Colombia. Greek deities have been a popular subject for artists for thousands of years.

may be influenced by the geography of the country in which a civilization lives. Mount Olympus, a towering mountain in Greece, became known as the home of the gods in Greek mythology. The top of the mountain was so high and so unreachable to the Greeks that they said the gods and goddesses must live there.

Like other ancient cultures, the Greeks also created myths to help them make sense of natural **phenomena** that they could explain in no other way. For example, the Greeks did not understand why earthquakes occurred. A story about the god Poseidon punishing his enemies by shaking the ground underneath them offered Greeks an answer. Poseidon was also believed to control the sea. His changing moods could explain why the sea was calm one day and stormy the next.

Greek myths have been passed down for thousands of years. There are several ways we have learned about them. One is through written works, such as books or plays, that were created by later cultures based on stories from ancient Greece. These works have survived and are still enjoyed today. We have also learned about ancient Greek myths through artwork such as sculptures and paintings. The Greeks sometimes told their myths in the form of art. For example, sometimes they made **mosaics** depicting, or showing, important myths. They also decorated vases and other containers with stories of their heroes, heroines, gods, and goddesses. Even Greek coins were often decorated with images from myths. Many Greek sculptures still exist today in museums. We can even see some floor mosaics in their original locations. Hopefully, like the stories they tell, these works will be preserved for years to come to give future generations an authentic look into the mythology of ancient Greece.

Uranus is the only planet that is named after a Greek god rather than a Roman one.

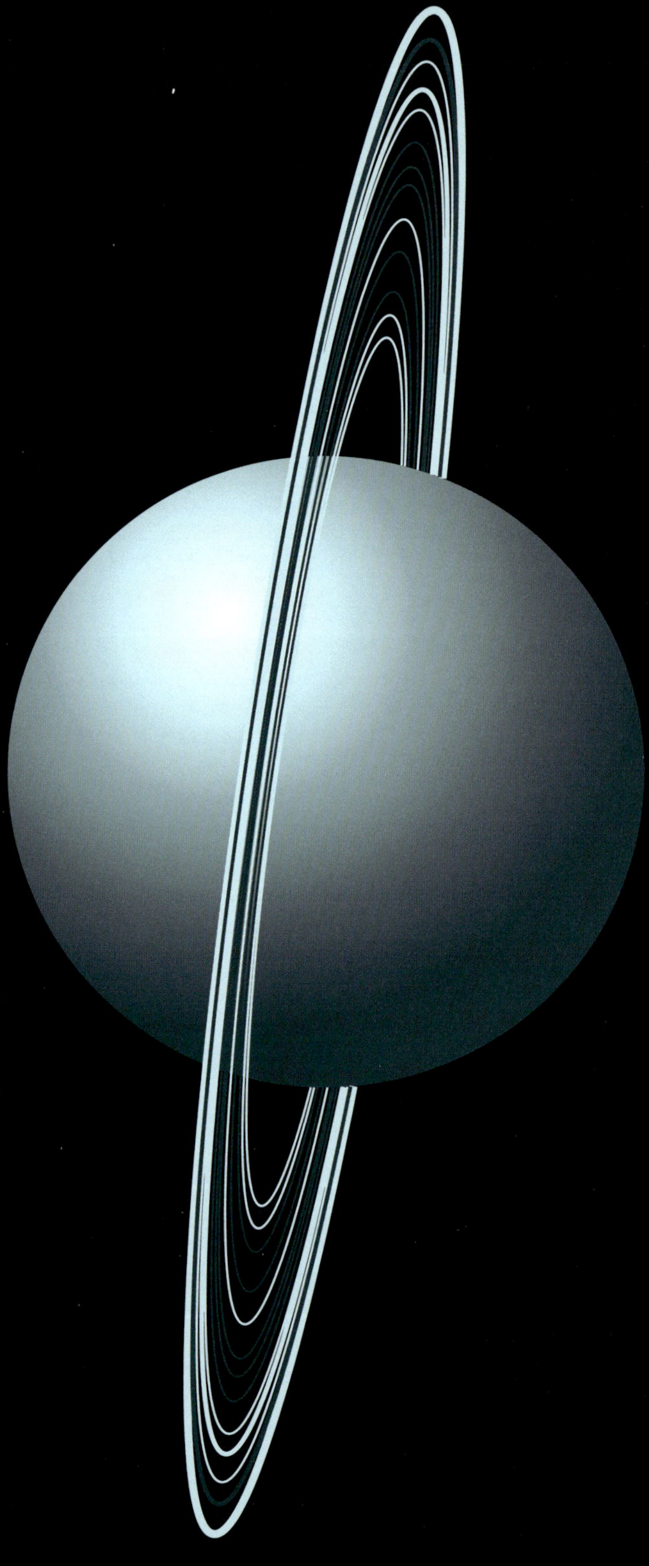

CHAPTER ONE

Creation Stories

Nearly every culture in the world has at least one myth about how the world and everything in it came into being. Many cultures have more than one story. This makes sense when we remember that a main function of mythology was to help ancient cultures explain the natural world in a way they could understand. Without the **sophisticated** tools we have today, it was hard for early cultures to perform accurate experiments, although many did try to gain a more scientific understanding of the world around them.

The Titans

This myth comes from the Theogony*, a work of mythology written by a Greek poet named Hesiod.*

In the beginning, there was **Chaos**, which was a dark, swirling void. Eventually, things began to emerge from Chaos, such as Gaia (Earth), Uranus (Heaven), and Tartarus (the Underworld). Gaia and Uranus came together, and Gaia gave birth to giant monsters: three Cyclopes, who had only one eye each; three Hecatoncheires, who had 50 heads and 100 arms each; and twelve Titans—six brothers and six sisters, all humanlike giants.

Uranus hated his children and shut them away in Tartarus. However, Gaia worked with Cronus, one of the Titan brothers, to come up with a plan. Cronus fought with Uranus and wounded him, and the blood that splashed on Gaia made her pregnant. This time, she gave birth to the Erinyes, also called the Furies, who were underworld goddesses of **vengeance**; the Giants, a strong and aggressive race; and the Meliae, who were nymphs, or nature spirits who lived in ash trees.

With Uranus defeated, the Titans ruled the universe, with Cronus as their leader. Some took control of the sea, while others ruled the sun or the moon. Eventually, Cronus married his sister Rhea. Together, they had six children. As each of the first five was born, Cronus swallowed them because Uranus had warned Cronus that one day his children would do to him what he had done to Uranus, and Cronus did not want that to happen.

Rhea was greatly upset by this, so when Zeus, the sixth child, was born, she hid him in a cave. To fool Cronus, she gave him a rock wrapped in cloth. Cronus grabbed it and swallowed it whole, thinking it was his child.

Zeus grew up and eventually learned about his brothers and sisters, whom Cronus had swallowed. He wanted to set them free. Gaia helped Zeus give Cronus a strong medicine to make him throw up. Out came the stone Rhea had told Cronus was baby Zeus, along with Zeus's five brothers and sisters: Hestia,

Variations

In some versions of this story…

- Everything in creation starts with Chronos, or Time.
- Gaia gives birth to the Giants because she is upset that Zeus and the other Olympians have overthrown the Titans.
- The group of Titans includes the children of some of the original twelve Gaia gave birth to.
- A goddess named Metis, who later becomes Zeus's first wife, is the one who gives Cronus the medicine that makes him throw up.

This picture shows Zeus holding lightning bolts and standing on top of a defeated Cronus.

Demeter, Hera, Hades, and Poseidon.

Zeus led his siblings in a 10-year battle against Cronus and the other Titans. Eventually, two of the Titans—Prometheus and Epimetheus—decided to help Zeus. They advised him to free the Cyclopes and Hecatoncheires from Tartarus. When Zeus did this, the Cyclopes were so thankful that they gave him lightning bolts he could throw as weapons. They gave Hades a hat that would make him invisible, and Poseidon got a three-pronged spear called a trident.

After a long, fierce battle, Zeus's side won. They sent the Titans to Tartarus and began their rule of the universe from the top of Mount Olympus, giving them the name "the Olympians." Prometheus and Epimetheus were the only Titans who were not banished because they had helped the Olympians.

◆ ◆ ◆

This story explains the creation not only of the universe, but also of the gods. Hesiod did not invent the stories in the *Theogony*; he simply wrote down myths that had, until that point, only been passed down orally. As his poem is one of very few ancient texts that have survived to the modern day, he is often credited with the story. However, shorter writings by other authors have also survived and show small differences in the story. Different translations of the work have also produced different versions.

The Creation of Humanity

This myth gives one version of where humanity came from and explains how the world came to be the mixture of both good and bad that we know today.

After the Olympians won the Titanomachy, or war against the Titans, Zeus gave Prometheus the job of creating people. Prometheus shaped them out of clay, and Athena, Zeus's daughter and the goddess of wisdom, breathed life into the clay men.

Prometheus gave Epimetheus the job of giving all living things on Earth special **attributes** that would help them survive, including speed, strength, sharp claws, wings, and fur. Unfortunately, when Epimetheus got to humans, there was nothing good left. For this reason, Prometheus made men walk upright like the gods. He also gave them fire so they would be able to rule over all the other creatures on Earth.

Prometheus loved the humans he had made even more than he loved the Olympians, who had overthrown his brothers and sisters and banished them to Tartarus. He wanted to take care of the humans. When Zeus announced that men must offer part of every animal they ate to the gods as a sacrifice, Prometheus thought that was unfair, so he decided to trick Zeus. Prometheus presented Zeus with two bundles wrapped in hide, or animal skin. One bundle contained bones and fat; the other contained the best cuts of meat. Prometheus told Zeus to choose which one he wanted as his sacrifice. Zeus picked the one with the bones, and because he had given his word that he would accept whatever he picked, he could not change his mind.

Zeus was so angry about being tricked that he took fire away from humanity. Prometheus stole it back by lighting a torch on

The Flood of the World

Many ancient religions and cultures had stories of a flood that covered the world. The ancient Greeks were no exception. Their myth has to do with a different version of the story of humanity's creation. In this story, Cronus created the first humans before he was overthrown by the Olympians. These humans were called the Golden Race and they lived easy, perfect lives. The Golden Race eventually died out but continued to watch over the next race. This race, the Race of Silver, was childish and fought a lot. Zeus, who was by then ruling the universe, sent them to Tartarus and created a new race.

These new humans were very aggressive. They were called the Race of Bronze, and they fought even more than the Race of Silver had. The Race of Bronze was the first to introduce war to the world. Finally, the gods got so tired of the humans' evil actions that they sent a huge flood to wipe out humanity. Most versions say that there were two survivors of the great flood: Deucalion and his wife, Pyrrha. They survived because Deucalion, with the help of Prometheus, built a wooden chest. In it, he and Pyrrha sailed on the rising waters for nine days and nights. Eventually, they reached Mount Parnassus.

To thank Zeus for sparing them, they made sacrifices to him. Zeus rewarded them by letting Deucalion and Pyrrha create a new race of people to inhabit Earth. To do this, they threw stones over their heads. When the stones landed, Deucalion's became men and Pyrrha's became women.

the sun and bringing it to Earth. Zeus became even angrier and decided to punish both Prometheus and men. Prometheus's punishment was to be chained to a rock high in the mountains. Every day, an enormous eagle ripped out Prometheus's liver. Every night, Prometheus's liver grew back. After thousands of years of this torture, Heracles set Prometheus free by killing the eagle.

To punish men, Zeus created the first woman. Each of the gods and goddesses gave her a gift, so they named her Pandora,

This statue of Prometheus holding fire can be seen at Rockefeller Center in New York City.

which means "all gifts." Athena taught her how to weave and cook. Hermes taught her how to speak well and be tricky. Zeus gave her a large box filled with more gifts. He told her, however, that she should never open it.

Pandora knew she must not open the box, but one day her curiosity got the better of her. When she took the lid off, out flew terrible things, including sickness, poverty, jealousy, and revenge. Pandora closed the box as quickly as she could, but it was too late. All that was left in the box was hope, which was supposed to comfort humans in the face of the evils that were now loose in the world.

◆ ◆ ◆

This story explains many things about ancient Greek culture and beliefs. First, it provides an explanation for the creation of humanity and how people learned how to use fire. Second, it warns of the danger of upsetting the gods. Zeus's rage in the story was so great that he punished Prometheus and all humans in ways that persisted for thousands of years. The Greeks cared a lot about keeping Zeus and the other gods happy through worship and sacrifice, and this myth helps explain why.

Shown here are the remains of a temple dedicated to Zeus in Athens, Greece.

Zeus's choice of sacrifice also explains an ancient Greek practice. Greek priests would sacrifice an animal on an altar in a god's temple. The bones and fat would be burned so the smoke would float up to heaven and please the gods, and the worshippers would eat the meat.

Prometheus's trick showed how deeply he cared for humanity because at that time in Greek history, meat was very expensive. These acts of worship were the only time in their lives most people would be able to eat meat.

Think It Through

1. Why do you think Zeus imprisoned the Titans instead of destroying them?
2. Why do you think flood stories are so common among different cultures and religions?
3. How would having fire give humans mastery over other animals?

In the past, Mount Olympus was too dangerous to climb, and most people had no reason to try it. In modern times, with better equipment and the rise of hiking as a fun activity, many people have climbed to the "home of the gods."

Chapter Two

The Olympians

Most Greek deities lived on Mount Olympus, which is a real mountain in central Greece. They lived an easy, pleasant life there. They knew they were not going to die, so they were in no rush to do anything. They never had to worry about food or shelter. However, despite their easy life in heaven, the gods and goddesses were very competitive. They fought with each other often, and they could be cruel and nasty to each other and to humans. They were often jealous of each other, and each wanted to be more powerful than the others.

Hephaestus and Aphrodite

This is the story of how the god of metalworkers married the goddess of love.

Hephaestus, the son of Hera and Zeus, was the god of metalworkers and craftsmen. The other gods thought he was very ugly. In fact, Hera was so disgusted by how ugly her son was that she threw him off Mount Olympus. Hephaestus hurt his leg in the fall, and after that, he walked with a limp.

Hephaestus landed on the island of Lemnos, where a man named Kidalionas taught him how to be a blacksmith. After learning this trade, Hephaestus returned to Mount Olympus.

Using his new skills, he made Hera a beautiful golden throne. Hera took it as a sign that Hephaestus had no hard feelings about being thrown off the mountain. However, when she sat down, she realized the throne had been part of his revenge: She was tied down by invisible cords. Hera begged Hephaestus to set her free, but he refused.

Dionysus, the god of wine, took Hephaestus aside and got him drunk, then convinced him to set Hera free. When Hephaestus walked back over to the throne, Zeus appeared and asked Hephaestus to free Hera. Instead of telling his father that he had already decided to do this, Hephaestus made a bargain with Zeus. He said he would only set Hera free if Zeus would give him Aphrodite, the goddess of love and beauty, as his wife. Zeus agreed.

Aphrodite was not happy to be Hephaestus's wife. She began to see Ares, the god of war, behind her husband's back. Unfortunately for Aphrodite and Ares, Hephaestus caught them one day. He threw a net he had made of chainmail over them to trap them, then invited all the other deities over to laugh at them. Poseidon eventually convinced Hephaestus to release Aphrodite and Ares. Hephaestus

Variations

In some versions of this story...

- Hephaestus has no father; Hera gives birth to him on her own.
- Hephaestus is born with a bad leg that causes him to limp.
- Hephaestus limps because, when he tries to break up a fight between Zeus and Hera, Zeus throws him off Mount Olympus.
- Hephaestus lands in the ocean, where two sea nymphs teach him how to make jewelry with coral and pearls.
- Hephaestus has someone else take the throne to Mount Olympus, and when Zeus offers Aphrodite to anyone who can free Hera, Hephaestus returns to do so.
- Helios, the sun god, tells Hephaestus that Aphrodite is cheating on him.

This statue of Hephaestus shows him making a helmet out of metal.

and Aphrodite divorced after that, and Hephaestus married a goddess named Aglaea.

◆ ◆ ◆

This ancient Greek coin features a picture of Ares.

Myths were often used in ancient cultures to reinforce society's values or to teach lessons. Many experts believe that the lesson in the story of Hephaestus and Aphrodite is that people should not marry for the wrong reasons. The two were very mismatched, and the marriage was forced. Trapped in a marriage with a man she did not love, Aphrodite turned to another man.

The story also shows how divorce was treated in ancient Greece. Surviving legal texts show that either a man or a woman could ask for a divorce, and there did not seem to be much judgment passed on divorced people unless one of them had caused a **scandal**, as Aphrodite had by cheating with Ares.

The Role of Deities

The ancient Greeks worshipped many gods and goddesses, who served many functions for the Greeks. The Greeks looked to them for guidance. For example, the god Apollo was associated with music, so musicians would make special offerings to him to ask for his help.

A god might represent a part of nature. For example, Poseidon represented the sea, so sailors would ask him for help on their journeys. A god or goddess might also be identified with a particular city-state; for example, Athens was named after Athena. Gods and goddesses could help humans—if they felt like it—by giving them special powers or tools. This is known as divine intervention. Usually, though, deities didn't bother getting involved with humans. In general, they would intervene in human affairs only when it served a particular purpose for them. They often used humans to enact revenge against another god or goddess.

When gods and goddesses interacted with humans, it was only in certain ways. The humans always had to remember their place, which was beneath the gods or goddesses in terms of power. Any humans who didn't were punished.

Athena and Arachne

This myth shows how vengeful the deities could be.

A woman named Arachne was one of the best weavers in the world. She made beautiful items, and she was an expert at the craft. Many people praised her skill and told her she had been blessed by Athena, who was the goddess of weavers as well as wisdom. One day, the pride going to her head, Arachne boasted that her talent came from her, not the gods, and that she could weave even better than Athena. She challenged Athena to a contest to see who was the better weaver.

Athena disguised herself as an old woman and went to Arachne's house. She warned Arachne that Arachne should take

This picture from 1676 shows Arachne being changed into a spider.

back her boast, apologize to Athena, and admit that Athena was the better weaver. Arachne, not realizing who she was talking to, angrily said that she knew she was the best weaver and was ready to prove it any time. At these words, Athena changed back into her normal shape and agreed to the contest.

Arachne did not show her panic. The two women went to their looms and began to weave. Athena created a beautiful tapestry that showed how heroic the deities were. In each corner, she wove pictures of humans who had tested the gods and been punished as a result. Arachne, on the other hand, wove gods who had taken advantage of human women. She showed gods such as Zeus, Dionysus, and Poseidon changing their shape to either trick women or overpower them, and she included some of the women they had hurt. When she was done, Athena could not deny that the work was breathtaking.

Athena became very angry. According to some stories, this was because she had lost the contest; others say it was because of the subject Arachne had chosen. In her fury, she ripped up Arachne's tapestry and hit Arachne on the head with part of the loom. Arachne realized she had deeply offended the goddess and decided to hang herself in shame. However, just as she placed the noose around her neck, Athena took pity on her and turned her into a spider.

◆ ◆ ◆

Like most myths, this story serves multiple functions at once. First, it explains why spiders spin webs and why they have the name they do (*arachne* is the Greek word for "spider"). Second, it shows the danger of insulting the deities or challenging their authority. Arachne's boast and her decision to show the gods' sins bring the wrath of Athena down upon her. Although she was saved from death, Arachne and all her **descendants** were still punished by being turned into spiders. Part of the punishment was that, although Arachne could still weave, she no longer had the skill to make beautiful pictures.

Think It Through

1. Why do you think Hephaestus was the only god who was not described as having a perfect physical form?
2. Why did Hephaestus invite the other gods to laugh at Aphrodite and Ares?
3. Why do you think Arachne decided to show the bad behavior of the gods?

Achilles was a demigod whose mother held him by the heel and dipped him in the River Styx in the underworld. This made Achilles **invincible** everywhere except that heel. This statue shows Achilles pulling the arrow that killed him out of his heel. Today, when someone talks about having "an Achilles heel," they are referring to their greatest weakness.

CHAPTER THREE

Heroic Tales

The Greeks believed that heroes and heroines were somewhere between gods and humans. Often, they were demigods, or half-god, half-human. As Arachne showed in her tapestry, the gods spent a lot of time chasing after human women, and many ended up getting the women pregnant. Demigods were not as powerful as gods, but they were stronger in many ways than humans.

Just as myths are sometimes similar in many different cultures, heroes and heroines are often similar from culture to culture. Many of the Greek heroes and heroines share characteristics with heroes and heroines from other cultures and other times. For example, in most tales, heroes and heroines battle against some kind of danger or difficulty. In the end, the hero or heroine is victorious. Their victory usually helps the rest of society in some way.

Heracles and the Augean Stables

One of the most famous heroes of ancient Greece is Heracles—better known by his Roman name, Hercules. After being driven mad by Hera and made to kill his own sons, Heracles was told that he had to complete 12 tasks, or labors, to ***atone*** *for the murders he committed. This is the story of his fifth labor.*

This picture shows Heracles performing his 12th labor, which was to capture Cerberus, the three-headed dog that guarded the underworld.

Heracles was given the job of cleaning out the stables that belonged to a king named Augeas. Under normal circumstances, cleaning a stable would be no problem for a demigod like Heracles, but these were no ordinary stables. King Augeas owned more cattle than anyone else in Greece, and Heracles had to clean out thousands of stalls in only one day.

Augeas knew nothing about the 12 labors Heracles had been assigned. When Heracles arrived at Augeas's palace, he offered to clean Augeas's stables for him in one day in return for one-tenth of Augeas's cattle. Augeas laughed and agreed, thinking it was impossible for Heracles to make good on his promise.

Unfortunately for Augeas, Heracles was being helped by Athena. The goddess of wisdom gave him the idea to change the courses of two nearby rivers so that they flowed through the stables, taking all the dirt with them as they went. However, Augeas refused to give Heracles the cattle. In anger, Heracles killed Augeas.

◆ ◆ ◆

The son of Zeus and a human woman named Alcmene, Heracles was the strongest man in Greece. However, he was not perfect. He had a very bad temper and was not as smart as other Greek heroes. The stories of Heracles's 12 labors are still some of the most popular Greek myths today. Someone who does something that is seemingly impossible, especially involving physical strength, is sometimes said to have "performed a Herculean feat." This particular story shows that, although strength is a valuable trait, it is sometimes better to use wisdom. Another saying that could be applied to this story is, "Work smarter, not harder."

Variations

In some versions of this story...

- Athena does not help Heracles with his task, and it is his own idea to divert the rivers.
- Heracles only diverts one river.
- Heracles and Augeas take the matter to court, and the judge rules in favor of Heracles when Augeas's son says Augeas did promise Heracles one-tenth of his cattle. Augeas is so angry at his son that he banishes him from the kingdom.
- Heracles does not kill Augeas; he just leaves the kingdom.

Atalanta

Although most Greek heroes were men, there were also women who performed amazing feats.

Atalanta was a heroine well known for her bravery and hunting skills. After being abandoned in the woods by her father, Atalanta was raised first by a bear and then by a group of hunters. She was always comfortable in nature and, like her **patron** goddess Artemis, was a fearless hunter. She was also strong and brave, ready to face any challenge life threw at her. She was not interested in men or marriage; she wanted to be single forever, like Artemis.

In some versions of the story about Jason and the Argonauts—the crew who sailed with him on his ship, the *Argo*—Atalanta was a crew member and the only woman on board. She fought alongside the men and was treated as an equal. Because Atalanta was blessed by Artemis, the rest of the crew was blessed as well. One of the most famous stories about Atalanta's time with the Argonauts is about her wrestling match with a hero named Peleus, whom she defeated.

Another famous story about Atalanta is the hunt of the Calydonian boar. Every year, King Oeneus of Calydon held

This artwork illustrates a myth in which Atalanta kills two centaurs who try to force her to kiss them.

a party at which he made a sacrifice to the gods. One year, he forgot to include Artemis in his sacrifice. Enraged, Artemis sent a huge boar to terrorize Calydon. Oeneus invited heroes from all over Greece to come to Calydon to try to kill the boar. Atalanta was the only woman there, and at first, many of the men did not want to let her compete with them. However, a hero named Meleager was in love with Atalanta and wanted her to like him, so he convinced the rest of the men to let her join in the hunt.

Atalanta was the first to hurt the boar, and Meleager ended up killing it. He gave Atalanta the boar's hide as a gift, but his uncles took it away from her, saying a woman did not deserve such a trophy. Meleager killed his uncles, and when his mother heard that her son had killed her brothers, she killed Meleager.

◆ ◆ ◆

In stories, Atalanta is shown as equal to or even better than most men. In fact, her name means "equal in weight," with weight here meaning importance. Mythology often reveals the values of a culture, but it also often shows their fears or concerns. In most Greek myths, women are quiet, obedient, and not troublesome or independent. This reflected the way many ancient Greeks expected women to behave. Women were not allowed to vote, own property, or work outside the home. They were meant to keep house and serve the men in their life. Some city-states gave women more freedom than others, but the records that have survived to the present day do not show that any of them gave women equal status to men.

Most Greek myths were written down by men. The stories about Atalanta and other independent Greek women show the opinion that a woman who is in control of her own life causes trouble. This is why such stories often end in **tragedy**, such as Meleager's death. Even though the men in these stories were responsible for their own actions, the women around them were often blamed for the choices the men made.

Mythology and History

The Trojan War is the focus of many exciting myths. The war began as a result of the jealousy and competitiveness of the gods and goddesses. Their meddling caused a war between the Greeks and the city of Troy. The war raged for 10 years, and many heroes and heroines played a part in the war. The *Iliad*, an epic poem by a writer named Homer, tells about the exciting events of the Trojan War.

Historians are divided on whether the Trojan War really happened. Many ancient myths contain a grain of truth, so it is possible that the story started with a real war. More than one author has written about it, and some parts of their accounts are the same. Greek history stretches back so far that even some ancient Greeks were historians of their own culture. A man named Herodotus, who lived in the fifth century BCE, said the Trojan War had happened 800 years before he was born. Modern historians tend to believe that it is likely a war happened, but they doubt it lasted 10 years. They also do not believe some of the more magical or unlikely events that are recounted in the surviving stories.

One story in the *Iliad* says the Greeks hid inside a huge wooden horse, which they presented to the Trojans as a peace offering. After the Trojans brought the horse into the city, the Greeks came out and burned the city to the ground. Most historians believe that the city was really burned, but that there was no giant horse involved.

Odysseus and the Cyclops

This story comes from one of Homer's epic poems, the Odyssey, *about the Greek hero Odysseus's 10-year journey home after the Trojan War.*

This statue of Polyphemus's head was found on a Greek island called Thasos. It may have been made as early as the second century BCE.

Odysseus and his crew were sailing for home when they were blown off course by a storm. When they spotted an island, they landed there to try to find food. They were expecting to **forage**, so they were very surprised to find a large cave full of meat, cheese, and other foods, with a flock of sheep outside of it. Odysseus and his men ate until they were full, then fell asleep in the cave. They woke up when the shepherd—a huge Cyclops named Polyphemus—came home. He led his sheep inside, blocked the entrance with a rock, and then noticed the 12 humans in his cave.

Polyphemus immediately ate two of the Greeks, then fell asleep. In the morning, he ate two more. Then, he took his flock out to graze, making sure to block the cave entrance with the stone so the rest of the crew could not escape.

While Polyphemus was gone, the Greeks came up with a plan to free themselves. They found a log in the cave and used their knives to make one end very sharp. Then, they waited for the opportunity to use it.

That night, when Polyphemus came home, Odysseus offered him some wine he had brought with him from the boat. Polyphemus accepted, and when he asked who he was sharing a drink with, Odysseus replied that his name was Nobody. After several glasses of wine, Polyphemus was drunk enough to fall asleep. As soon as he closed his eye, the Greeks heated up the sharp log in the fire and drove it right into Polyphemus's eye, blinding him. He screamed in pain, and the other Cyclopes on the island came running to ask him who was hurting him. "Nobody! Nobody is hurting me!" Polyphemus yelled. The other Cyclopes shrugged at each other, told Polyphemus to keep the noise down, and went back to their own caves.

The next morning, Polyphemus let his flock out to graze as usual. He stood at the mouth of the cave, ready to catch any men who tried to escape. However, since he had been blinded, he did not notice that the Greeks were each clinging to the underside of a sheep. When they got outside, the Greeks let go of the sheep and ran back to their ship. As they sailed away, Odysseus shouted his real name back to Polyphemus. In a rage, Polyphemus threw a boulder at the crew, but missed due to his blindness.

◆ ◆ ◆

Homer's stories were very famous and beloved in ancient Greece. In fact, they helped form the backbone of modern Greek culture. Around 1200 BCE, Greek civilization collapsed, and the country fell into a dark age. The population decreased, city-states became more **isolated**, and even the written language was lost. When a new writing system was invented and Homer began writing down the myths people had been telling for centuries, the ancient Greeks were reminded that they shared a common history and culture. They began creating more works of art, and civilization built up again, bringing Greece out of its dark age.

Some ancient Greeks believed Homer's stories were true, and they tried to find the exact places where they had happened. Many agreed that the island of the Cyclopes was the modern-day island of Serifos, which has a large cave on it. Near that island is a smaller, rocky island, which the ancient Greeks said was the boulder Polyphemus tried to throw at Odysseus and his men.

Think It Through

1. Why do you think Augeas went back on his promise?
2. How does Atalanta go against the idea of how Greek women were supposed to act?
3. What can we learn from the story of Odysseus and the Cyclops about which traits Greeks valued?

The ancient Greeks decorated many household items, such as vases. Myths were a popular subject. This vase shows Odysseus blinding Polyphemus.

Chapter Four

Explaining the World

One important function of mythology in ancient cultures was to explain why the world was the way it was. Stories explained things such as historical events, natural phenomena, and important inventions. As Greek myths spread and their popularity grew, many people took inspiration from the stories to name objects, feelings, and more. In this way, some Greek myths are circular: They were created to explain the world, and the world was changed in small ways to literally reflect those explanations.

Narcissus

The story of Narcissus has had a lasting impact on the modern world in many ways.

Narcissus, a hero of the territory of Thespiae in Boeotia, was the son of the river god Cephissus and the nymph Liriope. A soothsayer, or fortune teller, told Narcissus's mother that her son would have a long life if he never looked at his own reflection. For this reason, Leiriope would not allow mirrors in their home. Narcissus grew up to be very handsome, and many human and divine men and women fell in love with him. Narcissus, however, rejected each of their advances, including those of the nymph Echo. Echo was so upset that Narcissus had rejected her that she eventually faded away into nothing but a voice.

Nemesis, the Greek goddess of revenge, learned about Narcissus's rejection of Echo. As punishment, she led Narcissus to fall in love with his own reflection. One day, he saw himself in a pool of water and immediately fell in love. He stayed by the pool for weeks, neither eating nor drinking, just staring at his reflection and wishing he could hold it. Eventually, he died of starvation.

Variations

In some versions of this story...

- Echo is cursed by Hera to only repeat the last words anyone says to her. Narcissus rejects her because he cannot have a conversation with her.
- Aphrodite is the one who curses Narcissus.
- Narcissus is not cursed by anyone. He simply falls in love with his own beauty when he sees his reflection.
- Narcissus kills himself with a knife because he cannot have his reflection. The drops of blood that fall turn into flowers.
- A young man named Ameinias falls in love with Narcissus, who sends him a sword as a symbol of rejection. Ameinias asks Nemesis to curse Narcissus before he takes his own life with the sword.

◆ ◆ ◆

The message the story of Narcissus gave to the Greeks, as well as to readers today, is that vanity, or inflated pride in your appearance, is a destructive trait. For the ancient Greeks, this was taken much more literally than it is today. The Greeks believed that reflective surfaces were windows to the future, and that looking into them for too long could trap a person's soul.

Many modern-day things have come from this one myth. The word "narcissistic" means "self-absorbed," and a personality disorder called narcissism includes symptoms such as an obsession with being beautiful or wealthy, feeling that one's self is more important than other people, and a strong desire

A daffodil is one kind of narcissus flower.

to be admired. A group of flowers called narcissi take their name from the story. Some people believe this is a reference to the flowers that grew when Narcissus killed himself in one version of the myth. Others say it comes from the fact that "narcissus" comes from the Greek word *narke*, or "numb," which means "unable to feel." Narke is the base of the English word "narcotic," which describes a drug that is used to numb pain. Too much of a narcotic can kill a person. In the story, Narcissus is numb to the feelings of others; in regard to the flower, the bulbs are poisonous.

Hermes and Apollo's Cattle

Most cultures have trickster gods. Hermes was the Greek trickster.

Hermes was making mischief almost from the moment he was born. His father was Zeus, and his mother was a nymph named Maia. Hermes was born in a cave at dawn. By noon, he had grown big enough to walk. Outside the cave, he discovered a turtle and scooped the turtle's body out of the shell. Across the empty shell, he stretched seven strings made from a sheep's gut. His new creation was a musical instrument called the lyre. After playing the lyre for a while, he was bored and ready for a new adventure.

Spotting a herd of white cattle nearby, Hermes decided to play a trick on the owner of the cows. He stole the cows, leading them away from their pasture. To disguise his tracks, he tied bundles of branches and reeds around his feet. He made the cows walk backward so the owner would not be able to follow their footprints either.

What Hermes didn't know was that the cattle belonged to his half-brother Apollo, who was also a

One of Hermes's roles was to be the messenger of the gods. For this reason, he is often shown as having wings on his helmet and his shoes.

son of Zeus. Apollo was the god of **prophecy**, so he knew who had stolen his cattle. He didn't know where the cattle were, but he knew where to find Hermes.

Apollo went to the cave where Hermes had been born. There he found Hermes hiding in his cradle, pretending to be a day-old baby. By this time, he was already full grown, so Apollo didn't fall for his trick. Apollo demanded to know where Hermes had taken his cattle. Hermes could tell Apollo was angry and tried to calm him, still pretending to be an innocent baby.

Apollo didn't play along, but he was amused by Hermes's cleverness. He took Hermes to their father, Zeus, who ordered Hermes to return the cattle. Hermes agreed and decided to give Apollo his lyre to make him less angry. Since he was also the god of music, Apollo was thrilled with the gift. He decided to let Hermes keep the cattle, and Zeus made Hermes the god of herds.

Hades and Persephone

This is the story of how Hades, the god of the underworld, married a goddess named Persephone.

Demeter, the goddess of the harvest, had a daughter named Persephone. Hades fell in love with Persephone the first time he saw her. He kidnapped Persephone and brought her to live in the underworld with him as his wife. Not knowing what had happened to her daughter, Demeter looked everywhere for Persephone. She wandered Earth, but was unable to find her daughter. Finally, she went into a temple and stayed there. While she was in the temple, crops all over the world stopped growing. Zeus realized this was causing a problem for humanity, so he ordered Hades to send Persephone back.

Hades knew he had to obey Zeus, but he could not bear to let Persephone leave him forever. Before Persephone left the underworld, Hades gave her four pomegranate seeds. For each one she ate, she had to spend one month in the underworld.

Every year, Persephone returns to her husband for four months. During this time, Demeter becomes sad again and does not help the crops grow. When Persephone comes back, Demeter is happy again and goes back to her duties.

◆ ◆ ◆

The ancient Greeks used this story to explain the changing seasons. The four months Persephone spends with Hades are winter. When she comes back, Demeter starts to pull herself out of her sadness, creating spring. Since Persephone's return signals the start of spring, the Greeks saw Persephone as the goddess of spring. In summer, Demeter is fully enjoying her time with her daughter. When fall comes, Demeter starts to feel sad, knowing she will lose Persephone again soon.

The ancient Greeks may have first invented myths as a way to explain the world, but as they learned more about science, they found other reasons for these natural occurrences. However,

This statue shows Hades taking Persephone to the underworld. In the Greek myth, he kidnapped her by splitting open the ground under her feet, causing her to fall to the underworld.

A Lasting Influence

Artists and writers have used Greek myths as inspiration for their works for thousands of years, and the stories have been reimagined many times. The Greek myths continue to be part of our everyday lives. There are television shows, movies, video games, books, graphic novels, and more based on Greek mythology. Characters from Greek myths are also used in advertising; for example, the Nike shoe company was named after the Greek goddess of victory.

New stories that are inspired by Greek mythology are being told all the time. The first book in the *Percy Jackson and the Olympians* series, written by Rick Riordan, came out in 2005. Since that time, there have been many more books, two movies, and a TV series based on this retelling of Greek mythology. *Hadestown* is a popular musical that is based on Greek mythology. A 2018 novel called *Circe* retells the *Odyssey* and some other myths from the point of view of the witch Circe, who is a character in the original stories. There is no doubt that Greek mythology will continue to be a constant presence in the modern world.

even people who did not believe the myths were real could still enjoy the stories and the lessons they taught.

This remains true today. Greek mythology invites us to embrace the timeless themes of heroism, sacrifice, love, and the search for meaning. Reading or watching them not only connects us to history but also gives us inspiration and guidance for our own journeys of discovery, both of ourselves and the world around us.

Think It Through

1. Do you think Narcissus deserved his punishment?
2. What can we learn from the story of Hermes and Apollo?
3. What are some areas where you can see Greek mythological influences on modern life?

GLOSSARY

atone: To do something to make up for a wrong that has been done.

attribute: A quality belonging to a particular person or thing.

chaos: Complete confusion.

descendant: Someone related to a person or group of people who lived at an earlier time.

dialect: A regional variety of a language differing from the standard language.

forage: To search for food or supplies.

invincible: Unable to be hurt or killed.

isolated: Set apart from other people or places.

mosaic: A picture made up of small tiles.

patron: A person or god chosen as a special guardian or supporter.

phenomena: Observable facts or events.

prophecy: A prediction of the future.

scandal: Something that offends accepted moral standards or disgraces those associated with it.

sophisticated: Very complicated and advanced.

tragedy: A disastrous event.

vengeance: Punishment in retaliation for a real or perceived injury or offense.

FIND OUT MORE

Books

Hamby, Zachary. *Greek Mythology for Kids: Legendary Stories of Gods, Heroes, and Mythological Creatures*. Oakland, CA: Rockridge Press, 2022.

MacCarald, Clara. *Greek Mythology Monsters*. San Diego, CA: BrightPoint Press, 2022.

Menzies, Jean. *Greek Myths: Meet the Heroes, Gods, and Monsters of Ancient Greece*. New York, NY: DK Publishing, 2020.

Tracosas, L. J. *Ultimate Greek Mythology: Adventurous Stories, Fun Facts, Amazing History, and Beyond!* New York, NY: Z Kids, 2023.

Websites

BrainPOP: Greek Gods

www.brainpop.com/socialstudies/ancientcultures/greekgods

Watch a short video and take a quiz to test your knowledge of Greek gods.

***National Geographic Kids*: "The Gods and Goddesses of Ancient Greece!"**

www.natgeokids.com/uk/discover/history/greece/greek-gods

Read about some of the best-known ancient Greek deities.

YouTube: Pirates Kidnap a Teenage God, They Live to Regret It

www.youtube.com/watch?v=ztsKDcnGVcM

Watch an animation based on an ancient Greek poem.

Publisher's note to educators and parents: Our editors have carefully reviewed these websites to ensure that they are suitable for students. Many websites change frequently, however, and we cannot guarantee that a site's future contents will continue to meet our high standards of quality and educational value. Be advised that students should be closely supervised whenever they access the internet.

INDEX

ABOUT THE AUTHOR

Johanna Barrow studied Classics at Tulane University. She fell in love with Greece when she studied abroad there, especially after participating in an archaeological dig. Today, Johanna divides her time between Greece and the British countryside. When she is not writing books, she can be found volunteering at Corde's Cat Rescue or curled up in front of the fire with a good murder mystery.